T0208093

THOUGH I DON'T DESERVE IT, GOD'S HAND OF PROTECTION WATCHES OVER ME

THOUGH I DON'T DESERVE IT, GOD'S HAND OF PROTECTION WATCHES OVER ME

My Story

A R T H U R   L U K E

THOUGH I DON'T DESERVE IT,
GOD'S HAND OF PROTECTION WATCHES OVER ME
MY STORY

iUniverse books may be ordered through booksellers or by contacting:

iUniverse
1663 Liberty Drive
Bloomington, IN 47403
www.iuniverse.com
1-800-Authors (1-800-288-4677)

ISBN: 978-1-4917-8139-5 (sc)
ISBN: 978-1-4917-8140-1 (e)

Library of Congress Control Number: 2015918227

Print information available on the last page.

iUniverse rev. date: 12/17/2015

About the Book

This is a true story showing how God protected a young boy from Georgia through life's ups and downs. God's hand guided the author, helping him endure diseases, near tragedies, successes, and joys. Each triumph increased his faith. Know that with God on your side, nothing is impossible. Obedience to the will of God allows Arthur Luke to continue serving him even after a stroke. This is the story of Arthur's life. The following are nuggets from the book that will interest the reader.

Should a Senior Citizen Adopt a Child?

After much prayer and direction, we both decided to adopt Savannah. Beautiful families are created when couples expand their families with adopted children. Scripture tells us in Psalm 128:3 that your wife will be like a healthy vine providing plenty of fruit, a spring of life in your home. Your children will be like young olive shoots, and you will watch them bud and bloom around your table.

After the sudden death of my nephew, Que, I preached his funeral. My Bible text was Matthew 20:1–19. The parable is about the vineyard workers who were hired at different times of the day but were all paid the same amount of money. This is the one thing that was different: out of a twelve-hour day, those who were hired at the eleventh hour were paid first. The first shall be last, and the last shall be first. The meaning of the scripture is that in the kingdom of God, the subject is the reward of willingness to serve, whether one comes early or late. We should be grateful, not envious, if permitted to work long and hard for our Lord. Greatness is not ruling over others but serving others.

My future is better than what happened to me in the past. God will see me through if I focus on him.

CONTENTS

Chapter 1

Rolling to California

I can remember that God was watching over me when I was young. My dad was in the military for over twenty years and was transferred to many places. In 1955 we flew to Munich, Germany, where we stayed for two years.

I was four years old and had to climb the steep stairs to get to our apartment. I would go to the store and get money for returned beer bottles. The snow was so cold, but I still liked playing in it. One day I fell down the stairs while carrying beer bottles, which required stitches. When my dad gave parties at night, I would wake up early and drink the remaining liquid in the bottom of the glass. This was not good to do, but it was what happened.

My mom and dad and their four children journeyed from Columbus, Georgia, to Los Angeles in 1957. I was six years old. On the way to our new home, our station wagon flipped over in a ditch. God's hands of protection were there with us. No one was hurt, the tow truck turned our car upright, and we continued our journey. We moved into a white brick house at 1650 West Twenty-fourth Street. The residence was only for two years, and we were on the move again to San Miguel, in Central California.

After my parent's divorce, it was hard on our family because there was only one income. My mother, Bernice, was a strong woman who kept us grounded in the church. I loved God, and this would shape my relationship in the future and my knowledge of what God can do. Trying to prove you could do things on your own can prove to be disastrous. Proverbs 3:5 says, "Trust in the Lord with all your heart and lean not to your own understanding." In all your ways, submit to him, and he will make your path straight.

We attended Second Baptist Church in Paso Robles. My mom was an usher and Sunday school teacher. Though there were struggles in our household, she knew that God would make a way out of no way. At this time there were now six kids total, three boys and three girls, in the house.

When I was eleven years old, I sang in the choir and went to Sunday school. I was baptized at this church. One year our church sent me to Los Angeles as a delegate to represent our church. I was so proud to be there, and this experience would shape my early childhood, helping me to remain committed and faithful to God.

One of the first songs I remember singing as a kid was "He Is the Light." Some of the words are, "He's the light of my heart, and I know that we will never part. He's the light of my heart, and we will sing and praise his name."

Proverbs 22:6 says, "Train up a child in the way he should go and when he is old he will not depart from it."

CHAPTER 2

MY HEAD HURTS

When I was a sophomore in high school, I started getting headaches and couldn't go to school because of them. I got the headaches from junior varsity football practice. It was during a tackling drill with my teammate, and we hit helmet to helmet. This violent hit was the reason I stayed home for a week

I went to the doctor, and after some tests, he said I had spinal meningitis. A place in Springville, California, treated this disease. I was there for eight weeks, and each day I had one of three treatments: an IV in the arm, a needle in the spine, or a needle in the back of the neck.

I kept up on my homework, and after completing my treatments, I returned to regular school. Some of my classmates thought I was going to die. Again, God had his hands of protection on me. Psalms 55:22 says, "Cast your cares on the Lord and He will sustain thee. He shall never suffer the righteous to be moved." After getting back home, my mom sacrificed to visit me every weekend, and my brothers and sisters welcomed me home.

CHAPTER 3

GRACE UNDESERVED

There was a terror in our low-income housing development in Paso Robles. Someone was breaking into apartments at night and stealing items, but thankfully no one was assaulted. The more the robber broke in, the more people became afraid.

Police were on the lookout for the robber, who wore a mask. Finally the man was caught, and we were surprised that the robber was captured. He deserved to go to jail for all the mental anguish he'd caused others. Then I thought about how God does not give us what we really deserve. Grace is God's unmerited favor. Grace is God doing good for us even when we do not deserve it. In the Bible, grace and mercy are two heads of the same coin. Mercy is God withholding the judgment or evil I deserve; grace is God giving me blessing or good that I do not deserve. Because of God's mercy, I do not receive the judgment of God against my sins; because of God's grace, I receive eternal life and a promise of heaven even though I do not deserve them. Both mercy and grace come to me through the Lord and Savior, Jesus Christ.

What a wonderful savior! Jesus died on the cross for our sins, and all he asks of us is to serve him and live a godly life. We are God's witnesses to the world. God makes witnesses, and the Lord Jesus makes fishers of men witnesses. A witness is always a fisher of men. A witness of God is always bringing people to Jesus and to the ways of God by the life he or she lives.

God wants people who can reveal to the world this person and his eternal purpose in Jesus Christ. If you let the Lord transform you, he will make you a tree of life. As you become a tree of life, you will win souls to the ways of God. You will be counted among the wise and will shine as a star throughout the ages to come.

Chapter 4

Graduated from High School

I graduated from high school in June 1969. I was very athletic and played football, basketball, and baseball. I was named athlete of the year in my senior year. I went to nearby Cal Poly, San Luis Obispo, home of Pro Football Hall of Fame Coach John Madden, of the Oakland Raiders.

I played baseball and had a financial aid scholarship. My junior year I broke a bone in my left wrist. My baseball career was over, but by going to college, I had a backup plan. I would use my business degree and get a regular job to start my career. I concentrated on my college classes and went to two summer schools with a tough major, accounting.

I got straight As in bookkeeping in high school and thought this was like accounting. Boy, was I wrong. I was the only minority in accounting, which was really hard. I saw many people change their majors in college, and they ended up staying there longer. In 1969, it was the height of the Vietnam War. I needed to keep a grade point average above 2.00. I was determined to finish college early, and so

I took nineteen units or more three times; that was usually five or six classes. I had to study every night, and it was probably the most difficult and stressful time of my life.

God sustained me. As the Bible says in Isaiah 46:4, "I will be your God throughout your lifetime—until your hair is white with age. I made you and I will care for you. I will carry you along and save you."

I graduated from Cal Poly in three and a half years, in December 1972. I interviewed for a job with Security Pacific Bank during my last quarter in school. I got the job and started work in January 1973. God does answer prayer! I thank God for the job and praise him as he watches over his children. God watches over us in tragedies, joys, and successes.

Chapter 5

Wedding Bells

When I was twenty-three, I was looking to settle down and find a wife. I had an idea of the type of woman I wanted. She would have to be pretty, goal oriented, educated, and a good mother. I would have to search hard to find all of that in one woman.

Many years later, I ran into my piano teacher from when I was eleven years old. Joan was living in Stockton, California. She told me her niece from Louisiana had graduated from Southern University, Louisiana, and had moved to California with her sister in Riverside.

I got her niece's address and drove out of town to meet the prospect. Brenda was as beautiful as advertised. I first met her in the summer, and she was wearing a bikini. The curves of her body were stunning as the water beaded up on her skin. We went on several dates, and I was getting serious about her. We got engaged and then married nine months later.

I was married on July 5, 1975, in Paso Robles to Brenda Cyrus. This was one of the happiest days of my life. I wanted to turn my life around and obey God because he had done so much for me. Deuteronomy 30:10 says, "If you obey the Lord your God and keep his commands and decrees, that are written in this Book of the Law; and turn to the Lord your God with all your heart and with all your soul."

I was active in the church as a Sunday school teacher and a young deacon. My church was Mt. Zion Baptist Church in Bakersfield. The pastor was Rev. A. L. Dirks.

In 1976, I was promoted to assistant manager in loans. Bakersfield was a small town that was hot with bad air quality. In 1977, after a dust storm, I contracted valley fever. The doctor said breathing in the spores from the ground caused the illness. I was sick for eight weeks. Rest was the cure for valley fever, and some people died from this disease. When I got well, my doctor suggested I leave this town. I interviewed for an assistant manager position with my bank in Sacramento. I did not realize that Sacramento was also a valley. In February 1978, I started my new job.

A month earlier, my daughter, Janiene, was born. Being a father and watching my child grow up was super. God added a joyous time instead of sorrow. Philippians 4:4 says, "Rejoice in the Lord always, I will say it again, Rejoice."

Chapter 6

Driving to Bakersfield

My sister-in-law and her three kids lived with us for two and a half years. The reason she lived with us was due to a serious accident. Living with us in Bakersfield provided a safe environment for her family while she healed from her injuries. God always has someone to help when you're in need of a helping hand.

Brenda was pregnant with our first baby, and I would be transferred to another branch in Sacramento. We would be coming back on the weekends so that Brenda could see her sister and the kids.

One Friday night after work, we decided to drive to Bakersfield. The banks closed at 6:00 p.m., and we got on the road after 7:00 p.m. The distance one-way was 270 miles. I quickly got tired after a long day at the bank, and so I pulled over twice and took a little rest and got back on the road.

We were thirty miles from Bakersfield, and then it happened. I was in the left lane and fell asleep. The car began to drift to the right shoulder, and when the tires hit the dirt, I applied the brakes. God watched over me and prevented an accident. This was another time that he rescued me.

Our family was in jeopardy and needed someone with power and authority to make a way out of no way. God is in control and loves his children. He watches over them, and 2 Timothy 4:18 says, "The Lord, will rescue me from every evil attack and will bring me safely to his heavenly kingdom. To him be glory forever and ever."

My two-year-old daughter, Janiene, who was in the car that night and survived that near mishap, is now thirty-seven years old and is a medical doctor. What a mighty God I serve.

Chapter 7

Adopting Phillip

Being a parent is one of the greatest experiences in the world. Watching a baby grow up and finally start walking is so uplifting. My daughter Janiene, was such a pretty baby, and it was a joy seeing her grow up. We were looking forward to having another child, but the years were passing by very quickly. Janiene was now seven years old.

Brenda and I decided to try to adopt. We met a little six-month-old boy at a foster agency, and we fell in love with him. There are many children in foster agencies who are looking for families to adopt them. If you have love in your heart for a child, I recommend this avenue. I believe God will truly bless you for sharing with one of his children. Psalm 127:3 states that "children are a blessing and a gift from God."

CHAPTER 8

DON'T SAY WHAT YOU WON'T DO

I was not looking to meet anyone new after my divorce in 1991. I felt bad about my part in the breakup of my marriage. Some things you wish would not happen. Most of this was my fault, and I was sorry.

My precious daughter, Janiene, asked me something that I never expected. A child always wants her mom and dad to stay together. She asked, "Can you ask Mom to get back together with you?"

I was mainly to blame, and I told her, "Brenda is going to say no."

Janiene asked, "But will you ask her anyway?"

I then asked Brenda if she wanted to get back together. She said no, as I'd expected, and I needed to get on with the rest of my life.

Life is full of ups and downs. Christians are overcomers and are able to come through many trials and tribulations with the help of God. 1 John 5:4 says, "For everyone who has been born of God overcomes the world. And this is the victory that has overcome the world—our faith."

My friend Leonard Feltus, who sang in the choir of our church, said he worked with a woman he thought would be just right for me. I told him I was not interested at this time. A month later, he told me she was a choir director, a good Christian woman, and he said I should I take her phone number and give her a call.

I finally called Sharon a month after that, and we went on a bowling date. We had things in common. We hit it off and got married nine months later, on November 20, 1993.

If you want to be used by God, then you will want to live a life before him that is right. You didn't need to be perfect; simply be someone who is attempting to live a godly life. 2 Chronicles 16:9 says, "For the eyes of the Lord run to and fro throughout the whole earth to show himself strong on behalf of those whose heart is loyal to him."

Chapter 9

God Calling

I was a dedicated church member at St. Jude Christian Tabernacle in Sacramento for over ten years. I taught Sunday school and sang in the choir. A very spiritual woman named Mother Potts spoke words over my life and told me I was going to be a preacher. I said that was not going to happen; God could use many other people who were more qualified than I was.

She kept telling me for months that God was calling me for the ministry and that I should accept my calling. I prayed to God and asked for direction, and despite my inadequacies, I accepted my calling. Matthew 28:18–20 says, "All power is given unto me in heaven and earth. Go ye therefore, and teach all nations, baptizing in the name of the Father, and the Son and the Holy Spirit. Teaching them to observe all things what so ever I have commanded you and, lo, I am with you always, even unto the end of the world."

If you have a problem, seek God. Go in prayer, and he will give you the solution for your life. I truly believe that, and God has shown it to me over and over. If you are faithful and obedient to his word, he will direct your path. There will still be highs and lows in your life, but God will sustain you.

I preached my first sermon in 2002. I was very nervous, but my mother, brothers, and sisters were there encouraging me. God brought me through this emotional time, and I thank him.

Whenever you are living for God's purpose, the adversary, Satan, will try to oppose you at every step. Early in my ministry, I developed a cough, and it was embarrassing. When I would talk I would cough. I asked God how I could preach if I had this annoying cough. The people would not be able to understand me. I prayed to God to help me, and he allowed me to preach without a single cough. When I finished preaching, I would start coughing again. This pattern went on for eight years, but each time God came to my rescue.

The knowledge of Christ can only be obtained through the word of God, and it is by that word that we distinguish between true and false. There are many false prophets and false teachers who claim to be preaching the word, and we must protect ourselves from the counterfeit. Matthew 7:15–20 says to watch out for false prophets. They come to us in sheep's clothing, but inwardly they are ferocious wolves. Do people pick grapes from thornbushes or figs from thistles? Likewise, every good tree bears good fruit, but a bad tree bears bad fruit. A good tree cannot bear bad fruit, and a bad tree cannot bear good fruit. Every tree that does not bear good fruit is cut down and thrown into the fire. Thus by their fruit, you will recognize them. True teachers of Christ display the fruit of the spirit: love, joy, peace, patience, kindness, goodness, faithfulness, gentleness, and self-control. Galatians 5:22–23 says, "False prophets and teachers display the acts of sinful natures. By these fruits we recognize real teachers and false teachers."

CHAPTER 10

SHOULD SENIOR CITIZENS ADOPT A TWO-YEAR-OLD?

There are many major decisions in your life, and I believe you need to consult and pray to God during these times. The decision that needed to be made was whether to adopt a two-year-girl named Savannah. Her two teenage brothers were in a foster home with the same agency for which we fostered for ten years.

I am from a single-parent home, and Sharon is from a single-parent home. After praying to God, we were split on the decision to adopt Savannah. I said yes; Sharon said no. Sharon felt we were too old for a toddler; we would be seventy-eight when she graduated from high school. Also, she said we would not be able to provide a young, active life for Savannah. I said there was no age requirement to love and take care of a child. Also, I didn't want her to go from foster home to foster home. I believed God and trusted he would provide for us.

After much prayer and direction, we decided to adopt Savannah. Beautiful families are created when couples expand their families with adopted children. Psalm 128:3 states that your wife will be like a healthy vine producing plenty of fruit, a spring of life in your home. Your children will be like young olive shoots; you will watch them bud and bloom around your table.

As of this writing, Savannah is about to celebrate her fourth birthday. She is attending preschool and learning many things. She has a tablet and knows her ABCs and numbers. She is tall and loves to talk. She always wants to help her mom and dad.

Sharon loves Savannah, and they sometimes dress alike when going to church on Sundays. God continues to watch over this family. If you believe and trust him, God will also take care of you.

It is very important to communicate how you feel, but you must remember everything is not about and what you want to do. I asked Sharon, who was originally against adopting Savannah, to put herself in our little girl's shoes. I asked Sharon, "Would you want someone to adopt you if you were Savannah?" She said yes. When Savannah is acting out and not listening, she will tell me, "Come and get your baby." But in my heart, I know Sharon loves that child so much. I praise God for a tender heart, and for the Holy Spirit within to guide us through our situations.

CHAPTER 11

AN UNUSUAL JOB

In 2008, the economy was in the dumps, and businesses were not hiring. I got a job as a counselor. The position was an overnight, stay-awake job from 11:00 p.m. to 8:30 a.m. I worked this job for six and a half years. At this time I'd had sleep apnea for seven years. When I got off work, I would go home, put on my sleep apnea mask, and go to sleep. This was a very hard job. I was watching male sex offenders between the ages of thirteen and eighteen. I needed to provide for my family, and quitting this job was not an option. I asked God for the strength and alertness to make it through each night.

I had bad eating habits while working this job and developed edema, a swelling of the legs. It is caused by extra fluid in the tissues. I was overweight, and at this time I tried diets to lose weight with no success.

Finally, I went to the doctor due to some nose bleeds. The first thing they checked was my blood pressure. My pressure was very high, and I had to stay in the hospital for three days until my blood pressure came down.

My job had vacation but no sick leave, so I had to get better quickly. I returned to work and took it easy.

I was under some pressure to help my older brother, Nolan, by paying back some money I had borrowed from him. He helped me when I needed it, and I was determined to finish paying him off. There is a biblical principle here. Christians must avoid useless expense and be careful not to contract any debts they have not the power to discharge. The scripture reference is found in Romans 8:13. "Owe nothing to anyone except for your obligations to love one another. If you love your neighbor you will fulfill the requirement of God's law." I was so happy to finish paying off my brother. Two months later, I would be in the hospital for good.

Chapter 12

Stroke Cometh

I was at home and had just finished dinner when I started feeling strange. I slid out of my chair, and everyone started looking at me. I remember saying, "I'm okay." I tried to lift myself up, and nothing happened. I tried, but I could not move my hands or body. My wife called 911, and an ambulance arrived to take me to the hospital. I was having a stroke.

It was called a hemorrhagic stroke. This occurs when a blood vessel ruptures, causing blood to spill into and around the brain; it creates swelling and pressure. This damages cells and tissue in the brain. After one month in the hospital, I was transferred to a rehab hospital in Vallejo. In a two-month period, I lost seventy pounds. I had been trying to lose weight with no success. I prayed to God to lose some weight, but I never expected to lose seventy pounds by having a stroke!

At the time of the stroke, my left arm and left leg would not move. I didn't know what to expect. The hospital food was lousy, and they woke me up at 5:30 a.m. to take medicine. Also, there were rehab exercise classes to attend from 9:00 a.m. to 4:30 p.m. When I got to my room, I would be so tired. I would eat and sometimes go to sleep. However, I thanked God for being alive. God had spared my life again. In John 10:27–30 Jesus said, "My sheep hear my voice and I know them, and they follow me, and I give them eternal life, and they shall never perish; neither shall anyone snatch them out of my hand. My Father, who has given them to me is greater than all; and no one is able to snatch them out of my Father's hand. I and my Father are one."

I was given four weeks of rehab and a possibility to go home afterward. I had difficulty putting on my shoes and clothing with only my right hand and right foot. I was held in the hospital an additional three weeks until I had more mobility on my left side.

During my stay in the hospital, Sharon and Savannah would visit about twice a week. Even though they would only stay about three and a half hours, I was glad to see them. One day a flier came stating that a former stroke survivor was coming that night to tell her story. I attended that night and listened to a very inspiring story. Then I realized with God's help, I would recover too. I made a promise to myself that I would return to Kaiser Hospital in Vallejo to speak to stroke survivors and offer encouraging words. Romans 12:8 states, "If it is to encourage, then give encouragement; if it is giving then give generously, if it is to lead do it diligently, if it is to show mercy, do it cheerfully."

I want to thank all the people, churches, and loved ones who prayed for me while I was in the hospital. I received numerous get-well cards for my speedy recovery. I finally went home in a wheelchair on October 28, 2014. I was happy to be home, even though I had to move from our upstairs suite to the downstairs guest room. I could not walk. I was back to good home cooking, but my wife was under strict orders from my doctor to limit my food intake. They did not want me to gain back the seventy pounds that I had lost.

I went back to church after a long layoff in the hospital. I praised God for all that he had done for me. It was good to see my church members again and hear sermons. Psalm 104:33 says, "I will sing to the Lord as long as I live; I will sing praise to my God while I have my being."

In the next month at home, I would fall four times and not be able to get up even with assistance from Sharon. It was embarrassing to call my brother-in-law and his son to help me off the floor. Even with the weight loss, I still weighed 250 pounds.

When I woke up in the morning, I could not pull myself up with one hand. Sharon helped me lift myself up. I saw her laboring to lift me up, and so I tried something on my own.

I would lay on my back, swing my left leg over the side of the bed, and then move my right leg up and down. Then with my right hand, I'd hold unto the sheets. I would then do a pull-up and lift myself. I was so proud of just eliminating one less task my wife would have to perform. I saw the toll and stress on Sharon's face as she had to take care of our three-year-old and assist me with just about everything. Soon my son, Phillip, now age thirty, would come help for one week. My mother, Bernice, age eighty-two, then stayed for three weeks to assist my wife. Thanks to God for the help.

Chapter 13

Thanking God for Thanksgiving

We had Thanksgiving over our house, and my family came for dinner to see how I was doing. It was such a great meal, and we gave thanks to God for what he had done. It reminds me of scripture in Leviticus 22:29, "And when you offer sacrifice of thanksgiving to the Lord, offer it of your own free will."

God has done so much for me. When I fully recover in the next three months, I will return to Vallejo to tell other stroke survivors they can overcome their disabilities. This tight-knit group of therapists has that philosophy of "each one, teach one." Being in a wheelchair was hard on my bottom and my back. The therapist suggested sitting in a lounge chair to ease the pain. My random falls in the bathroom were eliminated when I had the disability bars installed. Oh, what a happy day after the contractor finished the work! Once I started sitting in the lounge chair, I would think of other things to do to get relief from the wheelchair.

I started walking with my walker to the door and back several times a day. As I got stronger, I walked to the mailbox and back. This little bit of exercise would be the key to strengthen my left leg. My left arm is slow to respond. My therapist told me that even with exercise, some arms do not fully recover. I will do all that I can do and let God do the rest.

On Thursday nights I go to men's Bible study. We study various books of the Bible and have a dynamic Bible teacher named Arnold Stalling. We have been together for seven years and pray for anyone who has a need. We ask God for the healing power of Jesus. The results of our prayers are amazing. We document God's answered prayers each week.

CHAPTER 14

GETTING BACK TO DOING GOD'S WILL

I had been active in teaching Sunday school and preaching before the stroke. Now, I was being encouraged to start teaching again. I enjoyed studying the Bible and researching various topics of study. Jesus Christ, our Savior, gave his all for us, and I wanted to give my all for him.

My mom, Bernice, had six kids and took care of all of us. She gave her all for us and sacrificed so we would be able to have things. I know how she was able to do this: trust and belief in God was the key. When you rely on the heavenly father, he will come through every time. I am a witness to what God can do. In our own strength we can do nothing, but with God's strength we can do everything. Faith cannot grow without trials. If our faith is to increase, then we must go through the fire to get there. One's faith cannot increase without problems, trials, and hardships. When a person asks God for more faith, that person is asking for an increased burden. It is the increased burden that strengthens me to carry a heavier burden down the road. Unshaken faith comes from having your faith shaken.

The problems in our lives are often blessings in disguise. We must learn to view them from this spiritual point of view. The greater the burden placed on us, the greater the faith required to hang in there. It takes faith to continue living for God when things turn for the worse in our lives. Exercising our faith will make us more mature and stable in the Lord, if we are patient and do not give up. Sometimes our faith falters for a while, but a righteous man who falleth seven times rises up again. I don't know of one Christian who is invincible. The key is to always get back up off the ground, brush off the dust, and do what you can to get back on track for God. Pray and ask God to help you. Proverbs 24:16 says, "For a man falleth seven times and riseth up again, but the wicked shall fall into mischief."

Chapter 15

God Speaks

Often through a combination of fasting and prayer, our hearts are clearer and more sensitive to God. We may not hear God's literal voice, but his spirit confirms a certain direction or answer for us. Sometimes while praying, God's spirit will remind us of a scripture or truth in his word that we can directly apply to the situation. God will never contradict his word, and the message he gives will always bring joy to God. The Bible warns about adding anything to the already written word of God, or accepting any other messenger who claims to be superior to Jesus (2 Cor. 11:4).

I remember one Fourth of July, when I was a little boy. My father put my mother out of the car during an argument. This behavior upset me so much, and I learned how I didn't want to act. This had an effect on me, and I stopped drinking thirty years ago partly because of it. My father was the sweetest man when he was sober. When he was not, his behavior changed. Romans 13:13 says, "Let us walk properly, as in that day, not in drunkenness, not in lewdness and lust, not in strife or envy." I have seen so many lives affected by drunk drivers and the actions of people who drink alcohol. Young children are the ones most affected by this disease. If you love your kids, don't drink, because you might not be able to handle it and could hurt your kids.

As I prepare sermons, I ask God to speak to me and give me what he wants me to say to people. God does not force us to be used by him; it must always be a willing choice on our part. 1 John 1:9 says, "If we confess our sins, he is faithful and just and will forgive us our sins and purify us from all unrighteousness." You can go into a bathroom with dirty hands, and there is soap and water there, but if you refuse to use them, you will come out just as dirty as when you went in. You cannot blame the bathroom for that—you are to blame.

You can go to church and hear the truth of the word of God, but if you do not apply it to yourself, it does you no good. If you have not come to him, you cannot blame God because he has not given you all the good things he promises to those who come to him. You cannot expect to be used by God in beautiful ways unless you are willing to purify yourself and use the instruments he has provided.

CHAPTER 16

MOM'S LOVE—THE CLOSEST THING TO GOD'S LOVE

I grew up in the projects of Oak Park in Paso Robles, California. The low-income apartments housed over two hundred families. My mom taught us to keep our room clean, and she taught us to have pride in what we had. We had a limited income, so when I decided to take a girl to the prom, my lovely mom decided to make our outfits. She was an excellent seamstress and showed love to me and my date. This was very time consuming, but she came through.

My date's dress was made of the same material as my tuxedo. It was a shiny orange pattern, and we looked stunning. My mom told me that one didn't have to have a lot of money to look good. Love plus labor will outshine money each time. My mom has been a godly woman and my example for almost eighty-three years, and God continues to bless her after all these years. Her love goes beyond limits. God says in Isaiah 66:13, "As a mother comforts her son, so will I comfort you."

Next to God's love, the greatest love in the world is a mother's love. A mother never stops loving. A mother will never stop loving or praying for her child. My mother demonstrated her unconditional love to all of us. She stressed to us that we could be whatever we wanted in life, but it would take commitment and hard work.

CHAPTER 17
THE TIME IS NOW

I have started teaching Sunday school again, and now the next question is when I would preach again. I don't have a date when I will preach, but I am preparing now. God has placed in my spirit to be prepared. When you are humble, you are teachable and don't think you know it all. There is a parable in the Bible, in Luke 12:20, which says, "God said to him, 'You fool! This very night your life will be demanded from you. Then who will get what you have prepared for yourself?'" Preaching brings those to repentance, and the Holy Bible brings those to salvation. Can you see the reason a preacher needs to be ready to proclaim the gospel? There are souls at stake.

My nephew, Que, is a very humble man who was in the hospital with a leg infection. He has such compassion for others and loves his big sister, Eurydice. I am praying that he will recover and get better. God has the whole world in his hands, and his love for us is everlasting. When we allow God to use us, he directs those searching and yearning for salvation into our lives. The spirit of God today is drawing people to salvation. Our job is to find those to whom God is calling. Therefore, it does not depend on our abilities but availability. God will call us when the time is right.

It's our life that causes people to ask what makes us different. When we let the light of Christ shine through our lives, we demonstrate the love of God. Through our lives, people will be drawn to us when Jesus Christ shines through us.

I won't let a stroke hinder me or slow me down after God allowed me to recover. God is a good God and is worthy of praise. I trust and believe him. God has never let me down.

I am ready to preach again and have made preparations for my next opportunity. God has watched over me and raised me up for service. I want to express my faith to him through my willingness to be available.

My future is better than what has happened to me in the past. If I can get through those rough times and focus on God to comfort me, God will see me through.

CHAPTER 18

VOWS RENEWED

Sometimes events will happen in life where you wish you could get a second chance. You may get another chance, or it might pass you by. My wife, Sharon, asked me to renew our vows two years ago around our twentieth anniversary. I said no. It wasn't that I didn't want to marry her again. I thought we needed to be married longer in order to renew our vows. I know other couples who have been married longer, and they have not renewed their vows.

Boy, was I wrong. A relationship has nothing to do with what others have done or what you think. Tomorrow is not promised to any of us, and we need to live each day as if it were our last. Sharon felt bad about what I said, and so did I. Case in point: one year ago, I had a stroke. God brought me through my recovery. It gave me a new attitude. Now, out of the blue on June 12, 2015, she asked me if I wanted to renew our vows. This time I said yes.

Sharon is already making plans to find out if the local hall is available for November 20, 2015, for our twenty-second anniversary. Boy, am I in for some big expenses.

Sharon has been such a dedicated and faithful wife during these times. I love her for all she has sacrificed for me. This is another example of how the hand of God has kept me and watched over me. I truly am grateful and praise him every day.

Sharon asked if I would be able to walk down the aisle without the assistance of a cane. I said, "Yes, I will." My goal is to work hard. My plan is to start today. I asked my wife whether she'd be able to fit in that dress. She said, "My goal and exercise plan will enable a good fit in five months. May God be with us as we walk down the aisle of life together."

Chapter 19

Unexpected Storms

My wife, daughter, and I were going on vacation to visit my mother and sister in Paso Robles. One day after we started on this vacation, I got sad news that my nephew, Que, had died at age forty-six.

I couldn't believe it. Que had been in the hospital the same time I was there. He was large in size, weighing 450 pounds. He had many problems, but the main one was a leg infection. Que was a gentle, soft-spoken man who was always thinking of others. My earlier memories of him do not resonate with how I'm feeling. When life throws you curveballs, try to hit them up the middle. Que left his older sister, Eurydice, with the responsibility of completing his funeral arrangements. My family and I drove to the Riverside area to visit my son and daughter. We spent two days in Murrieta and two more in Riverside.

I got the word that I was expected to preach the funeral of my nephew. I never would have agreed to perform the service if I was asked, because I knew I would break up at an inappropriate time. The funeral was to be the following

Wednesday. There were events that were scheduled to happen before the funeral, such as a boat cruise. I did not understand why.

When everyone came to Morro Bay for the cruise, it was so good to see people whom I had not seen for many years. There were about twenty-five of us. A toast was made to Que's graduation photo, and there was his favorite food, macaroni and cheese. I found out later that it was Que's wishes to go on a cruise; now it made sense. The day of the funeral came, and we were five minutes late getting to the church. I hobbled to the pulpit with my walker, greeted the pastor, and took my seat next to him. I started crying when the obituary was read. I knew this would happen.

My Bible text was Matthew 20:1–19. "The parable about the vineyard workers who were hired at different times of the day, but were all paid the same amount of money. This is the one thing that was different: out of a twelve-hour day, those that were hired at the eleventh hour were paid first. The first shall be last and the last shall be first."

Que was always concerned about going to work and paying his bills, even if it affected his health. That was why I chose this scripture to preach his funeral. The meaning of the scripture is that in the kingdom of God, the subject is the reward of willingness to serve, whether one comes early or late. Christ is not teaching economies. We should be grateful, not envious, if permitted to work long and hard for our Lord. Greatness is in not ruling over others but in serving them.

As I got up to preach, I was nervous as always, but God allowed me to preach Que's funeral without tears.

After preaching and sitting down, my sobs returned. I never thought I would be able to preach, but God's help brought me through. May God rest your soul, Que, and I will see you on the other side in heaven.

Scripture References

1. Matthew 20:1–19
2. Proverbs
  3:5, 2
  22:6, 2
  24:16, 28
3. Psalm
  55:22, 3
  104:33, 24
  127:3, 12
  128:3, v, 19
4. Philippians 4:4, 9
5. 2 Timothy 4:18, 11
6. 1 John
  1:9, 30
  5:4, 13
7. 2 Chronicles 16:9, 14
8. Matthew 28: 18–20
9. Galatians 5:22–23, 17
10. Romans
  8:13, 21
  12:8, 23
  13:13, 29
11. John 10:27–30, 23

12. Leviticus 22:29, 25
13. Luke 12:20, 33
14. Matthew
  7:15–20, 16
  20:1–19, v, 38
  28:18–20, 15
15. Isaiah
  46:4, 7
  66.13, 31
16. 2 Corinthians 11:4, 29

Printed in the United States
By Bookmasters